How To Control Your
ANGER
(Before It Controls You)

Ron Potter-Efron

JOHNSON INSTITUTE
HAZELDEN®

How To Control Your Anger (Before It Controls You)
A Guide for Teens
Copyright © 1998 by Johnson Institute-QVS, Inc. First published by Hazelden 1998. All rights reserved. No part of this book may be reproduced or transmitted in any form or by any means, electronic, or mechanical, including photocopying, recording, or by any information storage and retrieval system, without express permission in writing from the publisher.

Hazelden Information and Educational Services
Center City, Minnesota 55012-0176
1-800-328-9000 (Toll Free U.S., Canada, and the Virgin Islands)
1-651-213-4000 (Outside the U.S. and Canada)
1-651-213-4590 (24-hour Fax)
www.hazelden.org

Printed in the United States of America

10   9   8   7   6   5

Library of Congress Cataloging-in-Publication Data
Potter-Efron, Ronald T.
  How to control your anger (before it controls you): a guide for teens / Ron Potter-Efron.
        p. cm.
  Summary: Describes anger, its possible causes, and suggestions for how to deal with it.
  ISBN 1-56246-179-6 (pbk.)
  1. Anger in adolescence—Juvenile literature. [1. Anger.]
I. Title
BF724.3.A55P67 1998
155.5'1247—dc21

                                                    98-3184
                                                       CIP
                                                       AC

Table of Contents

Do I Have an Anger Problem?

Is this you?

"I blow up almost every day about something. My parents won't give me freedom. School's a bore, and I hate the way they try to control me. My friends are great, but I even get into fights with them. Sometimes I feel like I'm going to explode."

1

Do you scream and yell a lot? Hit or threaten to hit? Does your anger get you into trouble at school? Have you lost friends because they got tired of your arguing and complaining? Do you often fight with your brothers and sisters? Do you have an anger problem?

If you do, you should know that too much anger can really mess up your life. You could lose your best friends—after all, who wants to be around somebody who gets angry all the time? Constant complaining and arguing at home, school, or work will only get you in trouble. But most of all, it's not much fun to be angry. Even though fights might be exciting, in between the fights, life can get pretty crummy if you're angry most of the time.

Everyone gets angry from time to time. Normal anger can even be positive if it helps you get busy to make things better. Normal, healthy anger can lead to healthy action.

Anger is healthy when:

+ It stays anger and doesn't turn into aggression (physical attacks).

+ You take responsibility for your feelings ("I'm angry," not "You make me mad.").

+ It's about issues and not personalities ("I need the car tonight," not "You're the worst parents in the universe.").

+ It only lasts a short time and doesn't grow into long-term resentments or grudges.

+ You can talk to those you are angry with without losing control (swearing, yelling, or saying things you later regret).

But anger isn't always healthy. Take the test on the next page to see how much control you have over anger. Place a check in each circle if the description fits you.

2

How Angry Am I?

○ I often lose control of my anger.

○ I say or do things when I get mad that I later feel bad about.

○ I hang on to my anger for a long time—I won't or can't let go of it.

○ My parents or teachers say I have an anger problem.

○ My friends/boyfriends/girlfriends say I have an anger problem.

○ When I get mad I really want to hurt someone.

○ I hit, shove, slap, pinch, or threaten when I get angry.

○ It feels to me like I'm almost always angry about something.

○ I try not to let my anger out, but then blow up anyway.

○ I believe other people are the cause of most of my problems.

○ Sometimes I can't stop arguing even when I want to.

○ It seems like people are always picking on me.

○ I say "I won't," or "You can't make me!" a lot.

○ I like scaring others by getting mad—that's how I get my way.

○ My anger is "all or nothing." I'm either furious or calm; I'm never just a little angry.

○ I've been suspended from school, lost jobs, been arrested, or gotten kicked out of my home because of my anger.

○ I enjoy being angry—that's when I feel excited, strong, happy, tough, really alive.

○ I argue with anybody in authority: teachers, parents, bosses, adults in general.

○ I often try to make others angry—to stir things up.

○ I often hate myself and do things that hurt me.

3

Count the number of items you checked and see where you fall in these ratings.

0-3 points. Cool! Unless you haven't been honest with yourself, you probably have no problem with anger at all. Go through the list again just to make sure you're not denying reality.

4-6 points. Not too bad, but you may have some stuff to work on.

7-9 points. Danger. You probably have problems controlling your anger, but not all the time. It could get worse unless you're careful.

10-12 points. Trouble. That's a lot of anger. Anger is definitely a real problem for you. Better get to work doing something about it.

13-15 points. Big trouble. Anger is taking over your life. It's time to get serious about changing how you express your anger before it's too late.

16-20 points. Disaster. Anger is wrecking your life. Almost everything you do is touched by your anger. Do you really want to live like this?

Here's another way to tell if you have an anger problem

You have an anger problem if your anger messes up any important area of your life, such as: friendships, family, dating, school, work, playing sports, health (such as hurting your hand by punching a wall), or driving.

Ever hear of the feelings bus?

You are the driver of the bus, and all your feelings are the riders—anger, sadness, fear, happiness, love, and even boredom ride along. If your anger starts driving the bus, you can expect a rough trip. Maybe you'd like to get off that bus for awhile or get back into the driver's seat. If so, keep reading.

Why Am I So Angry?

This question doesn't have a simple answer. In fact, there are many reasons why teenagers get caught up in being angry.

Common Reasons for Anger

Any of the following may contribute to angry feelings:

- growing up in an angry family

- believing that nothing seems fair

- having adult responsibilities but no freedom

- the desire to make your own decisions

- sexual development

- angry friends

- angry enemies

- alcohol and other drugs

- pride and power

- not liking yourself

Growing up in an angry family

It's hard growing up in an angry family. When parents are angry a lot and don't know how to express their anger in a healthy way, kids don't learn how to handle their anger either. Dad may hit, threaten to hit, or just yell a lot—so might Mom, brothers or sisters, grandparents, uncles and aunts. In some families, just one person gets mad a lot, and everybody else lives on edge trying to keep the peace. In other families, everyone bullies each other, with no one listening to how others in the family feel. When it does get quiet in an angry family, the quiet doesn't last for long. Everything is seen as a problem, but none of the problems ever get settled.

People in angry families tend to look for reasons to get mad at each other. They are suspicious of one another, thinking of the rest of the family as opponents, not team-mates or people they can count on.

7

Do you live in an angry family?

Even if you do, you can still learn to be less angry. But you'll need to talk with people *outside* your family—people your age and older who aren't always so angry. Look for role models of people who handle their emotions well. Ask them how they stay calm. Spend some time with their families if you can. That way you can learn how to handle your anger and can talk with others about it without blowing up.

Believing that nothing seems fair

Your mom tells you she'll give you ten dollars for watching the kids for a couple of hours. Then she doesn't get home until late afternoon. You're stuck home all day when you could have been with your friends.

Your dad says you can take the car to the party. But then he changes his mind and won't even tell you why.

Even your friends let you down. They say they'll call but you never hear from them. They gossip about you and tell stuff to others that was supposed to stay private.

Friends promise to be honest and then lie to your face. Parents preach about trust and break promises. Teachers nag about responsibility but forget their own duties. The world seems to be made up mostly of fakes, phonies, and frauds. Maybe you didn't notice this stuff before, but you sure do now. And you get angry about it. Very angry.

It would sure help if people listened to you, but they don't. And it's hard to say what you want in ways others understand. All in all, life gets awfully frustrating when nobody seems to understand your thoughts or care about your feelings. Life just isn't fair!

Having adult responsibilities but no freedom

George's parents are divorced. He's the oldest of three kids who live with their mom. Mom has to work, but the only job she could find is from 3 PM to 11 PM.

George has to baby-sit after school. He doesn't get out often. His younger brother and sister resent that he is in charge. They won't listen or obey. Mom can't afford to pay George, either.

After awhile, George starts to feel cheated. Other kids his age have fun. They have time for themselves. He gets grumpy with his brother and sister. He fights with his mother all the time. He wants his freedom and he wants it now.

George isn't the only teenager who feels this way. Perhaps you also believe that you have too many duties and not enough freedom. Perhaps that's why you feel angry and resentful.

9

The desire to make your own decisions

For George, the problem is too much responsibility, but for other teenagers it's the opposite: They're not allowed to take on responsibility or to make their own decisions. In short, they're treated like little kids.

Independence. That's what being a teenager is all about—becoming an adult and making up your own mind. So what happens when others try to tell you what to do, say, or think? Maybe that's when you get angry, even furious: "Let me live my own life! Let me make my own mistakes! I know what I'm doing! Back off!"

Your parents understand this need for independence sometimes, but they've got their own job to do. They're legally responsible for you until you're eighteen years old. Besides, they don't want to see you get hurt. So even the best parents can't give you total freedom.

Conflict between teens and parents is inevitable. Your job is to race toward freedom. Your parent's job is to keep you safe, to slow you down a bit. It helps a lot if you can understand each other. It helps if you can sit down together, talk, and try to find a compromise.

Handle your feelings to get what you want.

But compromises are impossible when people are shouting at each other. That's why you've got to get control of your anger in these situations. Besides, you're not going to convince anybody that you can make serious choices by throwing a tantrum. You need to handle your feelings to get what you want.

Angry enemies

Nobody, not even you, is liked by everybody. We all have people in our lives who don't like us much—enemies, rivals, those who belong to other groups. When they are mad at you, you probably feel that you are expected to be mad at them. Maybe you'd like to stop fighting, but think you can't because they would laugh at you.

You may find yourself trapped into being angry even though it isn't fun anymore. It isn't smart, either. But how can you get out of it if others are always challenging you to fight?

You can get out of this reputation trap, but it will take determination and courage. You'll have to quit playing the tough guy. You'll need to be able to say something like this: "Sorry to disappoint you, but I've got more important things to do. I'm too busy to fight all the time." You'll also need to find some new sources of personal pride. It's important to feel good about what you do and who you are.

It's your choice. Just because you've been angry doesn't mean you have to stay angry, no matter what your friends or enemies expect.

Alcohol and other drugs

Some people turn to alcohol or other drugs to escape from feeling angry. This may work at first, but it doesn't take long before alcohol and other drugs eventually bring a person down, making the person feel even worse.

If you have an anger problem to begin with, alcohol or other drugs can lower your inhibitions. Inhibitions are those thoughts and feelings that keep you from doing things you might regret. Without them, you are that much more likely to do something out of anger that you'll get in trouble for or wish you'd never done. Maybe you will do something stupid at a party and feel embarrassed or guilty about it later. Then you get angry at yourself. If you drink again to get away from the anger or so you don't have to cope with your uncomfortable feelings, the same type of thing may happen again.

14

If you don't stop this cycle of using alcohol or other drugs early on, you may become chemically dependent. You may come to depend on alcohol or others drugs to help you escape all kinds of uncomfortable feelings.

Alcohol and other drug use will only make the problem worse.

The best way to stop alcohol or other drugs from making your anger problem worse is not to use them. Instead, work on the other things that are causing you to be so angry. If you're already having trouble controlling your urge to use alcohol or other drugs, speak to your parents, a high school counselor, or another adult you trust.

Pride and power

Perhaps you're angry so often because it's something you're good at. You may not be great at math, or making friends, or making money, but you sure know how to get mad. You're proud of your ability to tick people off. Or maybe you get your own way by being angry—by screaming, yelling, threatening, hitting, or just plain being grouchy.

It's not easy giving up this reason for getting angry. After all, it works, at least once in a while. You can push people around with your anger pretty well.

Still, this is crude stuff. Sure, you may get what you want, but probably you're also getting into a lot of trouble with this bully routine. It's like pointing a gun at someone. Yes, they'll do what you want. But the minute you put the gun down they'll grab it and blast you.

15

Anger can be used to gain power. But the gains are short term. If you want real power and control, the kind that comes when people listen to you because you have something good to say, then you'll have to stop pushing people around with your anger.

Not liking yourself

Many teenagers have trouble with self-esteem. They look in the mirror and see ugly pimples. They aren't doing all that well in school. They can't count on their friends. They feel like they're on emotional roller coasters. They say things like: "Nobody likes me. I don't fit in. I never will. I hate myself." Sound familiar?

Two things happen when you feel this way. First, you are angry with yourself a lot. You can't be your own best friend. You may even do things to hurt yourself or to ruin it when something good happens to you. The message to others is "Look at how much I hate myself. Just try to make me feel better."

Second, you may take your anger out on others. Instead of dealing with your own self-hatred, you try to push it onto someone else—"Hey, I'm OK. It's you who stinks." That sneer in your voice, the look of disgust—maybe you can make others feel as bad as you do, or worse. Then at least you won't be alone in your misery.

You must learn to accept yourself.

What can you do to like yourself better? Self-acceptance is the key. You have to learn to accept yourself, even though you aren't perfect or as good as you'd like to be. Learning to like yourself may take some time, and you may need help from friends, family, and counselors. Try to be patient with yourself and others. And take time to discover new ways to control your anger.

What Can I Do to Control My Anger?

Think of your anger as a badly built house. That house leaks a lot and is full of cracks and problems. You own the house and you can tell it's in serious need of repairs. Maybe it even needs to be torn down and replaced.

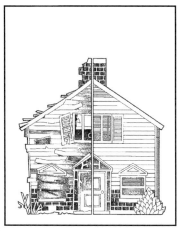

Fortunately, there are many tools you can use to become less angry. Some of the best ones are described on the next pages. They're good because they're quick, easy to use, and they work. But all the tools in the world can help you only if you actually use them. They won't do any good just sitting around in the tool box. That means your honest desire to change is more important than anything else. The tools are given here. Remember, though, that you are the carpenter in charge of the project. Only you can tear down your anger and build something better.

17

Here are some of the tools you can use to handle your anger:

- ☂ Be "selfish" about your anger.

- ☂ Take charge of your anger.

- ☂ Buy time.

- ☂ Stop the worst first.

- ☂ Don't RSVP every anger invitation.

- ☂ Challenge your angry thoughts.

- ☂ Put yourself in their shoes.

- ☂ Look under the covers.

- ☂ Learn to fight.

Be "selfish" about your anger

No matter who says you have an anger problem—your mother, father, teachers, friends, or counselors—the only opinion that counts is yours. Why? Because you won't change much until you decide that your anger is doing you more harm than good. Being selfish about controlling your anger means that you do it for *yourself*, so *you* can be happier and feel better.

Recovering alcoholics talk about getting "sick and tired of being sick and tired" before they were able to quit drinking. Are you "mad and angry about being mad and angry?" Have you had enough?

It's not easy to change the habit of being angry. You're going to have to think, talk, and act in new ways. Your family and friends may get in the way by expecting you to be angry just like you have been in the past. You may have to refuse to get angry despite their expectations.

19

You can choose to be angry or not to be angry. How do you know if it's time to stop being angry? Let's check it out.

First, make a list of the good stuff you gain by being angry, such as excitement, feeling powerful, getting what you want, knowing that people think you're tough, etc.

Now make a list of the costs of your anger—for example, troubles at home or school or with the law, lost friendships, headaches, endless arguments, lost privileges, driving tickets, accidents, fistfights, etc. Ask your friends for help with this list.

When you're done, compare your two lists. Think of the present—are you really happy with yourself this way? Think of the future—how angry do you plan to be next week, next month, or next year?

It's your choice. If you want to quit being angry—or if you are still making up your mind—read on.

Take charge of your anger

Have you ever watched people point their fingers during arguments? "It's all your fault," they say. "You make me mad."

Forget it. If you have an anger problem, you're the one making yourself angry, not others. Sure, other people do things you dislike. But so what? That's no big deal. It's you who won't take no for an answer or who won't stop fighting—you're the one. You make yourself angry.

You can't do anything about your anger until you take charge of it. Good or bad, it's yours. Your anger starts in your mind, takes over your body, comes out your mouth.

If you refuse to take charge of your anger, then others take over. Then your parents can make you mad any time they want so can the teacher you don't like, your boyfriend or girlfriend, your kid sister or your older brother. In fact, unless you control your anger yourself, just about anybody can push your buttons and make you mad whenever they want. So who do you want in charge of your anger—them or you?

21

Don't blame others when you get mad. How do you start taking charge? By telling yourself every day that you are in control of your anger. Quit blaming others when you get mad. If you have to point a finger, turn it toward yourself. Let them know, "This is my anger, not yours. You can't make me get angry. You can't make me stop. I'm in control. I'm in charge."

To many teenagers, anger feels like a speeding car racing along almost out of control. The trouble is, we don't have time to react at that speed. Too often we crash and burn. When this happens, we're in a state of rage.

Anger + Going Too Fast = Rage

We can't always stop the anger, but we can stop the rage. The best way to stop anger from becoming rage is by buying time. Ever hear of a voluntary timeout? That's when you decide to get out of a situation before you do something bad.

Timeouts work like this: When you can tell you are about to explode or hit somebody, you GET OUT NOW. Not in five minutes. NOW. Before you explode, not after. Leave the room. Get away.

If you have to yell and scream, go outside or to your room. Either of these is better than yelling at someone who might yell back or hitting someone who might hit back, which would get you into more trouble.

22

Do something physical, like running or walking fast around the block. Go shoot baskets. Talk to a favorite teacher. Write a letter to a good friend. You might even ask your parents to get you some big foam blocks to keep in your room. Then when you're really mad and need to let it out, you can throw them at the walls without getting in trouble for breaking things or hurting someone.

Once you let off steam physically, do something relaxing, like reading a comic book or a story. Don't get on the phone and complain about how miserable everybody else is and how mad they make you. Remember, your anger is about you and not them. Stay in control of your anger.

After you calm down, go back and try to talk things out. Timeouts aren't the same as running away from an issue; they're a chance to cool off before you have to deal with it.

"Okay," you say, "I can do that. But what if some adult is giving me THE LECTURE? They're mad at me. They won't listen. And I can't leave. They insist I stand there and listen to them."

That's when you have to take an *inner timeout*. Only you know you're doing this. It happens inside you. You concentrate on taking one calm breath at a time. You tell yourself you're not going to let this person sucker you into exploding. You put up a mental wall. You listen just enough to get the message. You tune out the rest.

23

Stop the worst first

Anger problems are like ladders that get taller with time. Over time, you have built rungs onto the ladder. Each rung is something you do when you get angry. At the top of the ladder is the worst thing you do, with each rung below being not quite as bad as the one above. One teenager's ladder looked like this:

| I hit my mother |
| I shove my brother around |
| I make fists and threaten to hit |
| I swear all the time |
| I make faces |
| I interrupt |
| I don't listen |

The goal is to get off the ladder. The way to begin is by climbing down from the top.

Before we go on, would you please fill in the rungs of your own ladder on the next page.

For now, let's just concentrate on the top rung. That's
probably the one that gets you into the most trouble. If
you could stop that one thing, life would get better.
Make a promise to yourself to stop that one behavior—
not that you will "try" to stop. Trying isn't enough. *Doing*
is what counts. Fill in the following line.

> ### Today, I promise myself that I will not
> _____, no matter what.

Then make the same promise again tomorrow and the
next day and the next.

Stop the worst first. Then start walking down the ladder.
Maybe first you had to stop hitting. Now you've done
that—no hitting for two weeks. What's next?
Threatening? Swearing? Running away when you're angry
and not coming back? Whatever it is, take the next step.
You'll find each one a little easier to stop than the one
before. Just keep walking down that ladder until you get
off it completely.

Don't RSVP every anger invitation

It's been a busy day. You've received invitations to go to three different places tonight, but you only have time for one. What do you do? You pick one, and say, "No thanks," to the rest.

Think of all the anger invitations you get every day: the alarm clock that wakes you up; your brother or sister hogging the bathroom; finding that you're out of orange juice or your favorite breakfast cereal; parents nagging about your homework; the bus coming early or late. And that's just the start of the morning.

An anger invitation is anything that you could choose to get angry over. But notice that word "choose." Angry people say "Yeah, sure" to a lot of anger invitations. So they're always mad about something. But for what? Who wants to be angry all the time?

You don't have to accept an anger invitation. You can say no. "No, thanks, I'm not going to let you bother me today." "No, thanks, I'll just have toast instead of cereal." "No, I choose not to get into that argument."

Figure that you'll get at least fifteen anger invitations today—fifteen chances to get upset. How many can you afford to accept?

Fishermen have a saying: SMART FISH DON'T BITE. You'll have to be a smart fish to get control of your anger. You don't have to take the bait just because it's out there.

Challenge your angry thoughts

Sometimes it takes only one thought to send a person into anger. These are called trigger thoughts; they push on your anger button, triggering you to get mad. Trigger thoughts can also be "automatic" thoughts—sentences, phrases, or feelings we pull up out of habit, without thinking about it. When a trigger thought is also an automatic thought, we think that thought, and POOF, we're mad. Here are some examples of trigger thoughts:

- ☙ Nobody understands me.

- ☙ I hate_____(my parents, homework, cats, kissing relatives, etc.).

- ☙ They can't make me.

- ☙ They're out to get me.

- ☙ It's not fair.

- ☙ I want it NOW.

- ☙ They can't do that to me!

- ☙ I'm an angry person, and I always will be.

- ☙ I can't help it; they make me mad.

We each have our own trigger thoughts. Take a minute and write down three of yours.

1 _____
_____

2 _____
_____

3 _____
_____

27

Now's the time to regain control over your own brain.
Here's how:

1 **Identify your trigger thoughts.** (You've already
done that.)

2 **Cut them off.** Take away their power. Stop them
from controlling you.

3 **Switch to new thoughts.** These new ones don't
make you angry.

Here's an example of how it works: One of Ellen's trigger
thoughts is "I never forget an insult!" A month ago, her
best friend Sally got mad and called Ellen a name. Now
Ellen's stuck. She can't forgive Sally. She can't forget. She
won't talk with Sally. And she really misses her friend.
What can Ellen do to get unstuck and be friends again
with Sally?

1 She needs to identify the trigger thought: "I never
forget an insult."

2 She has to cut it off: "Look, this is stupid. I'm just
hurting myself. I've painted myself into a corner. I
want to be friends with Sally again."

3 She has to switch to new thoughts: "I don't like
being insulted, but it happens. I insult others sometimes. I can let it go after awhile."

Now Ellen is no longer stuck. She can talk with Sally. She
can let go. She can be friends again.

Like we've been saying, it's up to you. You can
keep your trigger thoughts and stay angry, or you can
challenge them. You're in charge.

Put yourself in their shoes

Lately, your best friend Ralph has been acting like an absolute idiot. He said he'd come over yesterday and then never showed up. So today he promised again. "I'll come by about 6 o'clock," he said. And now it's 9 PM and he still hasn't shown up. Finally, you call him and he says he's sorry, but he's not coming over.

You're ready to strangle Ralph, aren't you? He has no right…And then he mentions that his parents are getting a divorce. And everything changes.

You're not mad at Ralph now. Instead, you know he's hurting. Maybe you remember a time when your parents separated, or when you thought they might. You can imagine how bad he feels. Now you're walking in Ralph's shoes.

29

It's hard to stay mad a someone when you walk in their shoes. But the time to do this is before you start yelling. That's when you can ask yourself these questions:

What's he or she so upset about?

Why is that so important to him or her?

What is he or she feeling right now?

It's easiest to put yourself in the shoes of your best friends, so start with them. Then go on to your brothers and sisters, or others who are like you. Then try your parents or teachers or people who are very different from you.

By now you may be thinking, "WHO CARES WHAT THEY'RE FEELING?" Well, if you really want to be less angry, you should. You'll be less angry when you take the time to understand where other people are coming from.

Look under the covers

Anger is a strong emotion; so strong it can even cover up other feelings, such as sadness, fear, and loneliness.

For example, you really want to do well this year in school, but you're having trouble in math. You just don't understand it. So you blow up in math class. You start throwing books around, swearing at the teacher, saying you won't study this stuff and no one can make you, that it's a waste of your time. Yes, you certainly are angry. But underneath the anger there are other feelings. What are they? Fear? Disappointment? Shame (feeling like there's something wrong with you)?

Here's another example. Your best friend is moving out of the neighborhood. You may never see her again. All of a sudden you are picking fights with your family. You're angry and frustrated that you have no control over the fact that your friend is moving. You're taking your anger out on your family instead of naming your *real* feelings: frustration, anger, sadness, loneliness, fear.

Anger is a feeling that can hide other feelings. It's like a huge blanket that covers up all the others. It hides your real feelings from other people, but also from yourself. Sometimes it's easier to be angry than to feel lonely, sad, or hurt. Sometimes it feels safer to be angry that to let people see your pain. Maybe you get angry to keep yourself from thinking about unpleasant or hurtful things, such as not making the basketball team, your parents' divorce, or your grandma's death. Perhaps you've gotten used to being angry—it's a habit. Or perhaps you told yourself you'd never cry and the only way you can stop is by getting really mad. Maybe people would care about you if you quit being angry all the time, and you're not sure you want to let them. Or maybe you live in an angry family where anger is the only feeling allowed.

Whatever your reason for using anger to hide your other feelings, you need to know that getting mad tells other people to keep away from you. Is that what you really want to say?

31

Try taking a peek under the covers. Find out what other feelings you have besides anger. Then start sharing those hidden feelings with others. Begin with the people you trust the most.

Then, when you start to get angry, ask yourself this one question: What else, besides anger, am I feeling right now? If you can take care of those other feelings, you won't have to get angry.

Learn to fight

No matter how hard you try, sooner or later you're going to get angry about something and you'll want to let others know how you feel. Here is a list of "Do's and Don'ts" that can help you express your anger without making matters worse. If you follow these rules you will probably get more of what you want.

don't

hit, push, shove, hold, or threaten

stand up and yell

make faces or make fun of others

swear or call people names

get stuck in the past

say "Forget it," "Tough," "Who cares," "So what," etc.

say "always" or "never"

interrupt

always have to get the last word

have to win every battle

do

sit down and talk

stick to one issue at a time

take timeouts before you lose control

listen—really listen—to what the other person is saying

slow yourself down—breathe calmly, relax

attack problems, not people

be open to discussion, bargaining, compromise

be flexible—able to change your mind if you want

be responsible for what you say and do

be honest about facts and feelings

Most of the "don'ts" are pretty clear. Hitting, swearing, yelling, name-calling, making faces, interrupting—all this stuff makes situations worse instead of better. So does saying things like "Tough," "Who cares," "You always do that," or "You never do this." Sure, all these things let people know you're angry, but that's all they are good for. You won't get what you want by acting that way.

It also doesn't do you any good to get stuck in the past. Let go of your old resentments and start over with people. Hanging on turns anger into hate.

Don't try to get in the last word or win every battle. When you do that, you're just arguing for the sake of arguing. Then others do the same and nothing gets done.

The "do's" are important. They turn arguments into discussions, no-win situations into both-win situations. We've mentioned some of them before: taking timeouts, slowing down, listening, stating your feelings, taking responsibility for your own actions (not making excuses). Let's look at some of the others.

33

> **First, stick to one issue at a time.**

If you're trying to defend your right to drive the car while your parents are trying to talk with you about your grades, neither one of you will get anywhere. You won't get the car. Your parents won't get through to you about your grades. First find a solution to one issue, then work on the next.

> **Second, attack problems, not people.**

It's okay to argue about an issue, but it's not okay to attack people. Keep to the topic. One "Oh, yeah? Well, your brain is fried, you stupid moron," leads to another. You may end up on top with the insults, but you probably won't convince the person you're arguing with that you're right about the issue.

34

> **Third, be flexible.**

Be open to discussion, bargaining, and compromise. The goal is to solve the problem that triggered your anger. Look for new ways to think about the subject. Be creative.

> **Finally, be honest about facts and feelings.**

If you want to stay out until 1 AM, don't tell your parents you'll be home by midnight. Also, be honest with your feelings. Tell your friends when you're upset with them. By the way, being honest is different than being crude or hurtful. Practice being honest and tactful at the same time. The truth, even when spoken in a whisper, is stronger than the loudest lie.

Nobody can make you follow these "do's" and "don'ts." It's entirely your choice. But if you want to use your anger well—if you want to solve your problems instead of making them worse—then these guidelines can help you get what you want.

Conclusion

It's not much fun being angry a lot. In fact, anger is really a pretty lousy feeling most of the time. Who would choose to be angry when they could be happy instead?

Here's a chance for you to decide to be less angry. As you see, there's plenty you can do to become less angry. Once you have it under control, you can even use your anger to help you solve your problems.

It's your anger. It's your life.

It's your choice.